Sign Language & Shapes

Bela Davis

Abdo Kids Junior
is an Imprint of Abdo Kids
abdobooks.com

Abdo
EVERYDAY SIGN LANGUAGE
Kids

abdobooks.com

Published by Abdo Kids, a division of ABDO, P.O. Box 398166, Minneapolis, Minnesota 55439.
Copyright © 2023 by Abdo Consulting Group, Inc. International copyrights reserved in all countries.
No part of this book may be reproduced in any form without written permission from the publisher.
Abdo Kids Junior™ is a trademark and logo of Abdo Kids.

Printed in the United States of America, North Mankato, Minnesota.

102022

012023

THIS BOOK CONTAINS
RECYCLED MATERIALS

Photo Credits: Shutterstock

Production Contributors: Teddy Borth, Jennie Forsberg, Grace Hansen

Design Contributors: Candice Keimig, Pakou Moua

Library of Congress Control Number: 2022937163
Publisher's Cataloging-in-Publication Data

Names: Davis, Bela, author.

Title: Sign language & shapes / by Bela Davis

Description: Minneapolis, Minnesota : Abdo Kids, 2023 | Series: Everyday sign language | Includes online
    resources and index.

Identifiers: ISBN 9781098264093 (lib. bdg.) | ISBN 9781098264659 (ebook) | ISBN 9781098264932
    (Read-to-Me ebook)

Subjects: LCSH: American Sign Language--Juvenile literature. | Shapes--Juvenile literature. | Deaf--Means
    of communication--Juvenile literature. | Language acquisition--Juvenile literature.

Classification: DDC 419--dc23

Table of Contents

Signs and Shapes.....4

The ASL Alphabet! . .22

Glossary...........23

Index 24

Abdo Kids Code.....24

Signs and Shapes

 is a visual language.
There is a sign for every
shape!

SHAPE

1. Make the "10" sign with both hands
2. Hold the hands out in front of the body with thumbs pointing slightly up and toward each other
3. Move the hands down toward the waist in a wavy, curvy motion

Kayla cuts her orange in half. It makes two circles!

CIRCLE

1. Hold the dominant hand out with the index finger pointed and palm facing down

2. Draw the shape of a circle in the air

James lays on his fluffy
pillow. It is shaped like
a rectangle.

RECTANGLE

1. Hold both hands out in front of the body with palms facing slightly down and index fingers pointed and touching

2. Draw a rectangle in the air by moving the hands away from each other, then down, then toward each other until the fingertips touch again

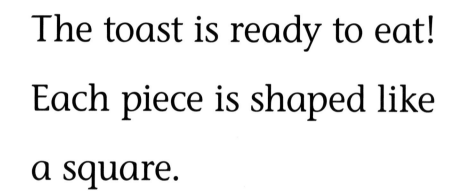

The toast is ready to eat!
Each piece is shaped like
a square.

SQUARE

1. Hold both hands out in front of the body with palms facing slightly down and index fingers pointed and touching

2. Draw a square in the air by moving the hands away from each other, then down, then toward each other until the fingertips touch again

11

The veggie pizza is yummy!

It is cut into triangle shapes.

TRIANGLE

1. Hold both hands out in front of the body with palms facing slightly down and index fingers pointed and touching

2. Starting at the tip, draw a triangle in the air by moving the hands down and away from each other, then toward each other until the fingertips touch again

Matt does a magic trick
with the ace of diamonds.

DIAMOND

1. Hold both hands out in front of the body with palms facing slightly down and index fingers pointed and touching

2. Starting at the tip, draw a diamond in the air by moving the hands down and away from each other, then down and toward each other until the fingertips touch again

Sam is making a flag out of paper. The last step is pasting on the stars.

STAR

1. Using both hands, extend both pointer fingers
2. Place the pointers next to one another
3. Brush them back and forth

Hailey has a heart-shaped balloon.

HEART

1. Hold both hands out in front of the body with palms facing slightly down and index fingers pointed and touching

2. Draw a heart in the air from top to bottom

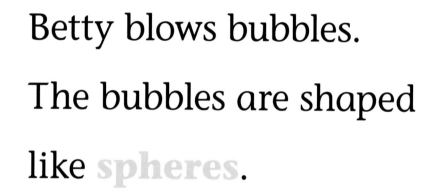

Betty blows bubbles.

The bubbles are shaped like spheres.

SPHERE

1. Curve both hands as if they are holding a ball and hold them out in front of the body with palms facing each other

2. The fingertips should almost be touching

3. Tap the fingers together a couple of times

21

The ASL Alphabet!

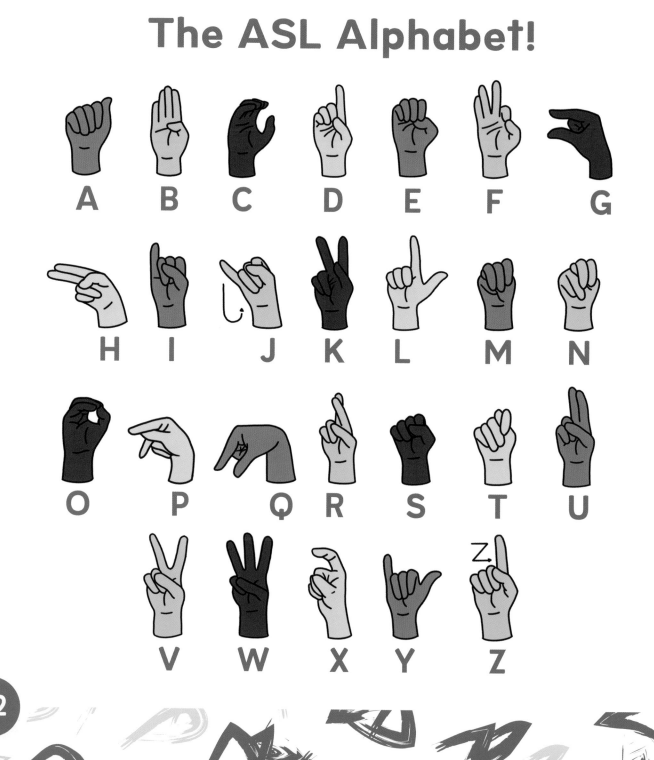

Glossary

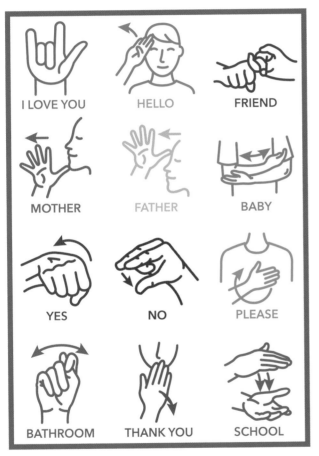

ASL

short for American Sign Language, a language used by many deaf people in North America.

pasting

causing to stick by means of paste, such as glue.

sphere

a round, solid figure in which every point on the surface is an equal distance from the center.

Index

circle 6

diamond 14

heart 18

rectangle 8

shape 4

sphere 20

square 10

star 16

triangle 12

Visit **abdokids.com** to access crafts, games, videos, and more!

Use Abdo Kids code

ESK4093

or scan this QR code!